I0759889

Edited by Kate Riggs Designed by Rita Marshall with Gary Kelley
Published in 2026 by Creative Editions P.O. Box 227, Mankato, MN 56002 USA
Creative Editions is an imprint of The Creative Company www.thecreativecompany.us
Photographs on pages 1 and 32 by Shutterstock (Love the wind)

Library of Congress Cataloging-in-Publication Data
Names: Winter, Jonah, 1962–author | Kelley, Gary, 1945–illustrator
Title: The burning of the books / by Jonah Winter ; illustrated by Gary Kelley.
Description: Mankato, MN : Creative Editions, 2026. | Audience: Ages 8-12 |
Audience: Grades 4-6 | Summary: "Reflecting on the Nazi book burnings,
evocative art emphasizes the threat of censorship, reminding us that what happened in
Germany could happen anywhere, even in America"— Provided by publisher.
Identifiers: LCCN 2025015372 (print) | LCCN 2025015373 (ebook) |
ISBN 9781568464114 hardcover | ISBN 9781568464121 ebook
Subjects: LCSH: Book burning—Germany—History—20th century—Juvenile
literature | Censorship—Germany—History—20th century—Juvenile literature
Classification: LCC Z659 .W56 2026 (print) | LCC Z659 (ebook) |
DDC 302.23/2094309043—dc23/eng/20250604
LC record available at https://lccn.loc.gov/2025015372
LC ebook record available at https://lccn.loc.gov/2025015373
First edition 9 8 7 6 5 4 3 2 1

Jonah Winter

The Burning of the Books

Illustrated by

Gary Kelley

CREATIVE EDITIONS

Once, in Germany, there was a book that changed the world:

the first major book in Europe
to be printed on a printing press.
The year was 1455.
The book was the Bible.

With the printing press, soon other books were printed.

Over time, there were libraries filled with printed books, books containing the memories and imagination and knowledge of human beings.

Many of these books were in Germany.
Germany was then a nation that valued education—and books.
Germans were free to read whatever books they wanted to read, free to think, free to question, free to learn.

BIBLIOTHEK

This was to change.

In 1933, the German government was taken over by a man
who declared his hatred for Jews
and his intention to remove Jews from Germany.

This new ruler made it a crime to disagree with him.
And he outlawed certain books, declaring them evil, dangerous.
Mainly books by Jews, but also books by Americans,
books that might cause people to think
or question him or his government—
these books were labelled "un-German."

Many German college students agreed with this label.
At student meetings, they spoke angrily about "un-German" books.
And they came up with a Big Plan:

In Berlin, the capital of Germany,
groups of students marched right into public libraries,
informing the librarians that they intended to remove
all books they believed to be "un-German."

The librarians assisted them,
as they went through the library, shelf by shelf,
removing thousands of books.

The students marched right into college libraries as well,
where professors helped them figure out
which books should be removed.

They marched right into bookstores—
removing books from the shelves.

The students carried the books out to the street
and loaded them into trucks.

And on May 10, 1933, the trucks were driven to a public square,
where the books were all dumped onto the ground—

thousands upon thousands of books
dumped into an enormous pile,
books that had only just recently
been sitting on bookshelves
or held in human hands.

Next to the pile of books
was a big pile of wood,
carefully stacked.

The sky turned black.
The moment had arrived
for something to happen.

It started with a parade—
large groups of students and government officials
marching through the streets with torches,

singing patriotic songs,
pledging their allegiance to Germany
and heading towards the square where the books were.

As crowds began to gather around the books,
students holding torches
set the pile of wood ablaze—into a raging bonfire.

And then it happened:
Someone threw a book
into the fire.

Within seconds,
the pages began to burn,
and what had been a book was now in flames, destroyed.

Some people cheered,
shouting patriotic slogans.
Some people looked on in horror, though,

as student after student stepped forth,
holding a book,
and made a pledge to destroy that book

then threw the book into the fire.
As book after book was thrown into the fire,
bands played music,

people gave speeches,
condemning the books
and praising the burning of the books—

books by Jewish authors,
but also books by non-Jewish Americans and Germans.
The burning of the books went on for hours.

By the time it was over,
and the pile of books was gone,
more than 25,000 books had been destroyed.

What happened in Berlin
also happened in 33 cities across Germany—
many on the very same night:
bonfires where thousands of books were burned.
By the end of the book-burnings,
at least 80,000 books had been destroyed—
no one knows for sure how many.

After the embers cooled,
and piles of dust were all that was left of the books,
the German government created a "blacklist"—
a list of authors who weren't allowed to be published
and whose books were banned from stores and libraries.

In the months following the book-burning,
hundreds of blacklisted authors departed Germany.
Many of them were Jewish.
Many of them moved to America, a nation

where people were free to read whatever books they wanted to read,
free to think, free to question, free to learn—
where people valued freedom of speech,
the right to say anything you want
and write anything you want.

What happened to these authors,
what happened to their books,
made its way into another book,
which you now hold in your hands.

And what happened in Germany
could happen anywhere.
It could even happen in America.

Author's Note

On January 30, 1933, Adolf Hitler was appointed Chancellor of Germany. He is widely regarded as the most evil person in human history, for having ordered the systematic murder of 6 million Jews and millions of other innocent people in an atrocity known as the Holocaust.

The coordinated book burnings led by the Nazi German Student Association on May 10, 1933, marked the beginning of the reign of terror conducted by Hitler's Nazi Party and their collaborators—and the beginning of their war on books: Between 1933 and 1945, the Nazis destroyed an estimated 100 million books. On May 10, some of the books they burned were by non-Jewish German and foreign authors, such as Thomas Mann, Oscar Wilde, and Helen Keller, though they mainly burned books by Jewish authors such as Karl Marx, Sigmund Freud, and 19th-century German-Jewish poet Heinrich Heine, who had famously said a century earlier, "Where they burn books, they will ultimately burn people." By the early 1940s, this frightening prediction would become a tragic reality in Nazi-run concentration camps.

People have been staging book burnings since ancient times all around the world. Even in America, whose government enshrines freedom of speech in its constitution, people of different political leanings currently engage in book burning, which is just one way of destroying books in our modem world. In the last several years, books deemed "offensive" by certain online mobs have been cancelled by American publishers because of social media pressure and/or fear of controversy—such that no copies of the books are available for anyone else to form their own opinions on. All acts of burning, cancelling, or otherwise destroying books come down to the same thing: to shut down not just the books but the people who write them.